Playmakers

Goalies

Lynn M. Stone

Rourke
Publishing LLC
Vero Beach, Florida 32964

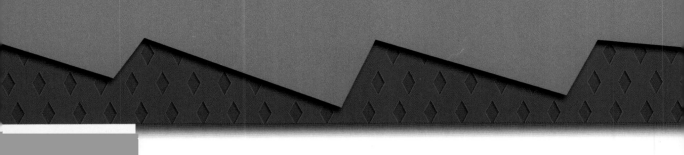

www.rourkepublishing.com

PHOTO CREDITS: All photos © Lynn M. Stone

Editor: Robert Stengard-Olliges

Cover and page design by Tara Raymo

Library of Congress Cataloging-in-Publication Data

Stone, Lynn M.
  Goalies / Lynn Stone.
     p. cm. -- (Playmakers)
  Includes bibliographical references.
  ISBN 978-1-60044-593-4
  1. Soccer--Goalkeeping--Juvenile literature. 2. Soccer goalkeepers--Juvenile literature. I. Title.
  GV943.9.G62S76 2008
  796.334'26--dc22
                                                    2007019103

Printed in the USA

CG/CG

Rourke Publishing

www.rourkepublishing.com – rourke@rourkepublishing.com
Post Office Box 3328, Vero Beach, FL 32964

Table of Contents

The Goalie

A goalie, or goalkeeper, is the last line of a soccer team's defense. The goalie is a specialized defender who positions him or herself close to the team's goal. The goal is a boxlike frame enclosed by a heavy net—except in the front. The goal box measures 8 yards (7.3 meters) across the front and 8 feet (2.4 meters) high.

Goalie

Like a cat watching a sparrow, a goalie's eyes follow the flight of an incoming kick.

A goalkeeper's job is to do whatever it takes to stop the opponents' shots from reaching the net.

A soccer team's objective is to score by kicking the ball into its opponent's net. The goalie's job is to prevent the kicked or **headed** ball from crossing the goal line and going into the net.

Goalies can legally use their hands to stop the flight of a ball on the soccer field.

The goalkeeper's position is unique on a soccer field. Unlike the goalie's other 10 teammates, the goalie almost never has to **dribble** a soccer ball. And the goalie is the only player on the actual field who can handle the ball with his or her hands. (Other players can throw a ball from the sidelines back into the field of play in certain situations.)

There are some limitations, however, on the goalie's use of hands. An area near the goal is designated as the penalty area. This area extends 18 yards (16.5 meters) onto the field from the goal line. A goalie can use his or her hands to deflect or catch a ball anywhere in this area.

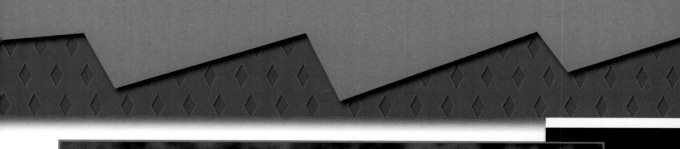

Once the goalie controls the ball, the opposing players cannot continue to kick it.

The Goalie's Skills

Most goalkeepers, especially at the upper levels of soccer, are highly specialized athletes. They usually play goalkeeper and no other position.

A goalie crouches, ready to spring.

Like a baseball **shortstop**, the goalie's basic position is a crouch, with hands ready to stop an incoming ball. Like a shortstop, a goalie must also be ready to spring from the crouch into full **extension** for a shot that is high or wide of where the goalie is positioned. Such defensive movement requires quickness and outstanding **eye-hand coordination**. Other soccer positions depend upon eye-foot coordination.

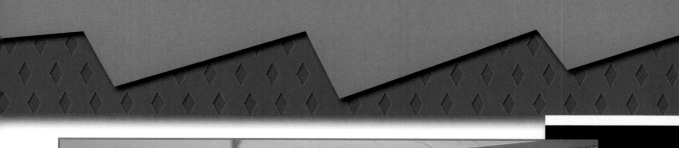

A goalie must be able to leap...

...and lunge to stop shots at the goal.

A goalie must also be able to neatly deflect the ball away or catch the ball. A goalie who drops, rather than catches, a kick may allow the kicking team a quick follow-up shot. By cleanly catching the ball a goalie stops the opposing team's attack, at least for the moment. Coaches like a goalie with "good hands," which means hands that are soft, **agile**, and strong.

A goalie deflects a shot that was beyond reach of being cleanly caught.

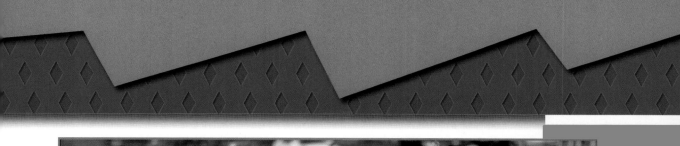

Sure hands are one of an all-star goalie's skills.

Gloves and the proper grip help a goalie secure a kick.

After stopping a kick on goal, a goalie must decide what to do with the ball. The ball can be **punted**, kicked from the ground, or thrown. A goalie with good kicking or throwing skills can accurately advance the ball to a teammate.

After a stop (save), a goalie punts the ball downfield, where it returns to play.

Rather than punt, a goalie elects to kick a ball on the ground directly to a teammate.

Goalies often punt the ball downfield in long, high kicks. A **booming** punt may be impressive, but it doesn't guarantee that the goalie's team will take possession when the ball lands. Punting can be helpful to kill time or quickly place the ball in an opponent's territory. It is important that a goalie have good ball distribution skills and make a wise decision about how and where to distribute the ball.

So, You Want to Be a Goalie?

As a goalie's hands make contact with a ball, an opposing player cannot continue to kick the ball. But there are tense moments when a kicker tries to beat a lunging goalie to the ball. Playing goalkeeper is not for someone with a weak heart or stomach for the possibility of unwanted contact. Among other qualities, a goalie must have a fearless attitude toward the job.

It takes courage as well as skill to stop an oncoming kick.

A goalie's fearlessness helps her make a point blank stop of a kick.

Quickness and height help a goalie punch away a high kick.

The most effective goalies are relatively tall, and they have good jumping ability. A tall goalie can stop a high kick that might sail over a shorter goalie's outstretched hands.

It's important for a goalie to communicate with other players. A goalie normally has a good overview of the entire field and the oncoming **attack**. The goalie can help position teammates more properly by barking commands.

From the goalie box, a goalkeeper studies the always shifting field of play and barks commands to teammates.

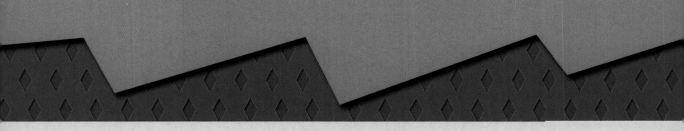

Glossary

agile (AJ ile) – refers to the ability to move quickly, easily, and with flexibility

attack (uh TAK) – a team's organized possession of a soccer ball as that team's players move toward the opposing team's goal

booming (BOOM ing) – high and long, such as a booming kick

dribble (DRIB uhl) – to quickly move a soccer ball and keep possession of it in a series of short kicks or taps

extension (ek STEN shuhn) – a leap or lunge to the maximum of one's ability

eye-hand coordination (EYE HAND koh OR duh na shuhn) – the ability to move one's hands skillfully in reaction and relation to what one sees

headed (HED id) – a soccer ball which has been intentionally struck by a player's head

punted (puhn TED) – a soccer ball which has been kicked by a goalie from his or her hands

shortstop (SHORT stop) – an infield position in baseball

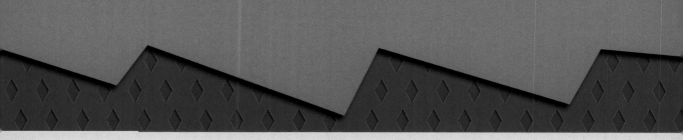

Index

Further Reading

DK Publishing Staff. *Soccer*. DK Publishing, 2005.

Gifford, Clive. *Soccer Skills*. Houghton Mifflin, 2005.

Peet, Mal. *Keeper*. Candlewick Press, 2007.

Website to Visit

http://www.jbgoalkeeping,com

http://www.soccerpracticebooks.com/gkbasics.html

http://www.soyouwanna.com/site/minis/mini/soccermini/soccermini4.html

About the Author

Lynn M. Stone is the author of more than 400 children's books. He is a talented natural history photographer as well. Lynn, a former teacher, travels worldwide to photograph wildlife in its natural habitat.